New Lease

Sandra Burnett

©Sandra Burnett 2016

Published by Otley Word Feast Press 2016,
OWF Press Community Company
9B Westgate, Otley, West Yorkshire LS21 3AT

All rights reserved. No part of this book may be copied, reproduced, stored in a retrieval system or transmitted, in any form or by any electronic or mechanical means without the prior permission of the copyright owner.

ISBN 978-0-9934275-2-7

Acknowledgements

'For the record' was awarded third prize in *Poems Please Me poetry competition 2015* and is published on line at www.poemsplease.me
'Her mother blames Jackson Pollock' was shortlisted for *The Frogmore Prize 2015* and is published in *The Frogmore Papers No. 86* (2015)
'I spend a morning with Billy Collins' was commended in *Red Shed Poetry Competition 2015*.
'Show' was published in *Prole issue 10* (2013)
'Lesson' appears in *Spokes – poetry on two wheels* (OWF Press, 2014).
'Sunflowers in Arles' was published in *A Mixed Bunch – The Flowers of the Washbur*n (Courthouse Writers, 2012) .

Thanks to Otley Poetry Gym and Courthouse Writers for their thoughtful and incisive comments on early drafts of some of these poems. Special thanks to Maura Dooley, Jane Kite, Gail Mosley, and Peter White for their encouragement, support and suggestions in putting this pamphlet together.

Contents

For the record	1
Escape	2
The return	3
The deal	4
My mother as a glass of water	5
Reunion	6
Lesson	7
Picasso's bicycle	8
Her mother blames Jackson Pollock	9
New lease	10
Show	11
Sunflowers in Arles	12
Witch's garden	13
Downsize	14
Eastwood Mill fire	15
Creation	16
Cowboy	17
Scaffolders	18
I spend a morning with Billy Collins	19
Sirens	20
Beaufort scale	21
Captives	22
Flight	23

For the record

He said she looked too innocent.
He could not capture his perfect shot.
I noticed only how she shivered.

From my bag of tricks I took Kohl
to outline her eyes. Did you see the photo
in the 1957 National Portrait Exhibition?

Those were the days when everyone
wanted a piece of her and some would say
I carved her up. No.

I was her trusted aide and conjured auburn curls
from next to nothing. Everywhere she went
my blend of sandalwood and jasmine lingered.

When I couldn't contain the signs of age
and her wealth had been snatched by bailiffs,
we shared my small flat in Greenwich.

I earned a modest living
holding an occasional séance.
She did not want for wine or cigarettes.

The day she failed to appear at breakfast
I found her in bed, bare-faced and wigless.
I worked my magic.

I shut her eyes, applied the make-up
and crowned her
with a mass of tight tonged curls.

The papers got it wrong.

I'll grant she died without a penny,
but since that freezing day
she'd been loved.

Escape

At first her prompt was enough to dislodge
odd syllables that tied his tongue.
Later, when two or three of his words knotted
she picked at them
like a mother removing lice eggs
from her child's hair until,
as if to hide from her fuss,
the ends of his sentences went missing.

She filled in the gaps.

For years she patched all he said
and just when it seemed
she had him stitched in her pattern
he caught at a thread and all
his hemmed-in lines unravelled
and he sang them out, gave them air,
let them slap at her cheeks
like the arms of his shirts she starched
and pegged out on blustery days.

The return

will be difficult
and it is wise
as you turn your key
to remember
there will be no shoes
in the hall to trip you,
no John Wayne drawl
from the living room TV
or familiar
That you, love?

Some suggest it's best
to head straight for the kitchen
and make a brew, provided you have
those one-cup tea-bags.
In the long term there's the issue
of your past,
how it lurks in drawers.

There may be a day
when you are spurred to search
for that lost Bradford & Bingley passbook
only to find his last list
of *To Do's.*

The deal

You will need to become as familiar to him as his shadow
and when his hand begins to quiver step-up, take his place.
Do not show a hiccup of grief. This is the moment
you employ his training.

Your remuneration will be
appropriately increased.

There can be nothing in writing.

My mother as a glass of water

My mother would not have been happy set alongside
a Murano or sleek Dartington. She would not have wished
to hold the gaseous liquid of a celebrated spring.
My mother was a squat tumbler and sat firm
while the worries of a parish poured into her.

My mother's glass was crafted by an apprentice glass-blower,
well versed in tradition but lacking in skill,
and so she was spotted with flaws of the kind
a portrait painter exploits to communicate the worth
of wisdom over beauty.

The water my mother held had gathered in clouds
on top of the Pennines then rained down to burst
the banks of the Aire and the Wharfe and my mother
filtered her water through all her beds of rocks, pebbles
and gravel, until its sweetness diluted arguments.

Even though my mother's glass was half full
she could not be drained.
Those who topped her up with sludge and salt
saw their work laundered to a dribble.

My mother refreshed anyone, regardless of age,
creed or colour, and you should forgive me
for believing her shatterproof.

Reunion

Winter has left us rusty
but soon we have the measure of the other's frame.
Pumped-up we hit the road
and rescue balance on every bend.
Masters of swerve
we take the hills for a freewheel down.
We push
through rush hour's haze.

Over the years
her knees, my brakes have been replaced
but still we crank the Dales
and time knocked off our personal best
is a secret kept
from those lycra gangs who pass then disappear
behind the horizon.

Built for comfort we're vintage sixties
and never forget the flowers to decorate
her helmet and my basket.

Lesson

We wheel your birthday present to the park,
a safe place to learn the art of balance.

Minus stabilizers I steady the bike while you,
biting your bottom lip, struggle to sit on the saddle.

I say,
> *Look straight ahead.*
> > *Grip the handlebars.*
> > > *Push on the pedals.*

I hold on longer than I should and have to ignore
my urge to sprint, catch you up

as your pace quickens. When you wobble, steer
a wild course, my heart brakes.

You remembered everything I said,
never looked back.

Picasso's bicycle

was blue and for a period his favoured means of travel.
When it ceased to be of use it was propped against a fence
and abandoned to the weather.

In the summer of forty-two,
left to entertain his daughter Maya, the artist
organised an afternoon sketching flowers.
But the child wandered off and chancing on the wreck,
she asked her father to take it indoors and make it better.

Whilst Maya ate her biscuits and drank milk,
Pablo set to work and when he said,
Look, I have made you a magnificent bull's head,
there were tears.

Her mother blames Jackson Pollock

Matilda thinks she lives under the sea
and when she is laid on her park bench,
looking up at the sky, her suns, moons
and stars are explosions of gloss.

Matilda thinks the lads that call her *Bitch*
are rubber ducks who will be lost to waves
even though they don't hurt her.
Sometimes they give her beer.

Matilda believes the *whoosh* she hears
is you and me, scudding past. She thinks
we are landfill being shoved this way and that,
'til we finally join a mass in the Pacific.

Matilda is searching for a wall
where she will paint her thoughts.
She has rescued two five-litre cans,
blue and yellow, from a skip.

Matilda will call her painting *Fathom.*

New lease

When the family's preference
turned to lentils, beans and carrots
the meat mallet played dead
amongst bent forks and crazed plates
and dreamed of being whisked away
by a fixer of strings on violins or a tuner of pianos.
The kind of artisan who would not dwell
on a bloody past.

But a mallet is a practical tool
and not designed to make the grade
in opera or ballet
so when it was grasped by a child
to add to his drum-kit
of discarded kitchen treasures,
it hammered out a rhythm
to make the dead dance.

Show

Gran's tea caddy was home for needles, white thread
and those cards of twelve shirt buttons.

Some nights she stayed up late turning Grandpa's collars
or cuffs; hiding frayed edges.

Rington's loose leaf was stored in a jam-jar on the cellar-head
next to her carefully stacked Royal Albert tea-set.

Mrs Cutts would take tea in the front room once she'd ticked
the rent book; she had an interest

in undersides of saucers and cups and Grandpa's
Vienna wall clock.

I had to light a fire and dust before her visit and Gran
would re-set a pair of filigree hands

to coincide with the 88 bus stopping at the street end.
Grandpa was in charge of winding up.

Sunflowers in Arles
(The housekeeper's tale)

He did not need absinthe those days
he walked the yellow wash of field;
selected fourteen seed-heads
with their merry-go-round petals.

Arms full, he fled to that sun-baked house
where, careless of formal arrangement,
(I thought he put too many in one vase)
he daubed and dabbed his rapid strokes
to catch our good Lord's light.

My bread, best cheese, he left
(I saw him swig the flowers' water);
all this before Monsieur Gauguin arrived,
and his moods began to darken.

I followed circling crows to withered fields
(I'm talking now of later in the year); found him,
lying in the midst of all those sapless sticks
with widow-heavy heads.

I slipped him Armagnac, kissed his sunken cheek,
turned his bandaged face towards the sinking,
red rimmed sun.

Witch's garden

Sorcery has brought me
to where we'd played
outside her gate, our games
of throw and catch.

Foxgloves had thrived
in her borders,
purple, white, mauve,
each throat rashed with plague

and in our childish spite
we'd picked Molly
to climb the fence,
retrieve our wayward ball.

That game stopped
when Molly disappeared.
The rumour was her family
did a moonlight.

Today concrete smothers soil
to home a car and caravan.
Plastic toys clutter a patio.
The Digitalis is gone.

Content that sand and cement bury
a legacy of menace I turn to leave
and spot, in the slip of earth
beside the fence,

a stem, heavy with blush bells.

Downsize

I took scissors to my sleeves.
I shortened them to your expectations.
I stitched side seams so no flare was left.

It is no longer the coat
I grew into and loved
for all the hidden pockets
a wife and mother has.

I cannot argue against the need for alteration
but on my shoulders this hangs heavy.

Eastwood Mill fire
(23 February 1956)

From her eighty years she takes one day
large as a loom that natters the din
of weaving sheds:

sifts through threads -

tea-break
shared cigarette
kiss on the neck;

machine oil
screams of *'fire'*
locked doors.

In this shortest month of the year
these remnants return to loom,
like a bale of shoddy,

in her thoughts.

Although this poem is about a fictional character a fire did occur at Eastwood Mill in 1956 and resulted in responsibility for the means of escape in factories being transferred from District Councils to the Fire Authority.

Creation

In truth
the Garden was mountainous.
Eve had a belly that celebrated pudding
whilst Adam was short and in need of a haircut.
The tree suffered from a fungal disease
and its fruit was bruised.

In telling
the Garden became tame.
Eve slimmed to size eight
and Adam displayed the benefits
of an improved diet and decent barber.
The tree was healthy.
The fruit waxed rosy.

Cowboy

When John Wayne strode into my front room
he caught his Winchester on the left door-jamb
and dislocated his shoulder.
I told him about the quack who'd fix it.
No cheques. No receipt.
He said, *Whisky, woman.*

From under the kitchen sink I grabbed
the Asda blend and poured him a slug.
He downed it in a gulp and was off
swaggering down the lane,
the gap between his legs begging
for a horse.

Like a shot I recognised a man with whom
I should have shared my Glenfiddich
and gave chase. I lost him
to the white van
on the corner.

Scaffolders

I found them in Yellow Pages
and they arrived in the prescriptive white van;
four men past being featured
in a charity calendar.

I'd been told to expect an "elite" team
and strong tea would be all they'd need
so their request for Paracetamol
unsettled me.

Between them they had a collection
of ceramic hips and dodgy knees
and I thought I'd been tricked into paying
for banter and bullshit

until a wagon arrived,
loaded with metal poles and wooden planks
and these guys raise a tower, moving like graduates
of The Yorkshire School of Dance.

I spend a morning with Billy Collins

He pours a second cup of coffee
and to distract from the neighbour's barking dog
plays Beethoven's Fifth, full blast.

It doesn't work and we take a walk.

There are frequent stops
to listen to birdsong and muse on reasons
for not keeping a gun.

He asks if I know of a good hotel
in Budapest.

Back at his desk, he scrawls
a snail-trail of foraged words and when he takes five
it is to listen to jazz and chop herbs.

He tells me about a study he has read
on congenital blindness
in mice.

He wishes me luck with my poetry.

Sirens

We had no interest in enticing the boozy crew
of that limp-rigged ship onto our rock.

Zeus, the niff of cheesy socks that wafted
ashore on the burps of zephyrs.

Only those with sheep-wool stuffed in their ears
could have thought our jeers a song of seduction.

We quickly roused a quarrelling quartet of Wind Gods
and watched them bully the vessel until, bored,

they set it on course for Ithaca
or some such dreary place.

In the wake of their storming, we spotted a little fellow
strapped to the mast and thought him dead,

though we later learned, he was responsible
for phantasmagorical tales

put about to pacify his wife following
an inexcusably long jaunt, with his mates,

to Amsterdam.

Beaufort scale

It is morning and I'm a **three**. Watch me
make mischief with Mirror dinghies.

By afternoon, and inland, I'm a **six going on seven**.
I bully umbrellas, floor dustbins, scatter their innards.

I gain force and mothers bolt doors at my rattle.
Tonight I'll be having your roof or chimney.

My gang of clouds will smother the moon
unless I allow them to scatter.

At an **eleven** my scream is a muster for warlords.
They'll beg me to whisk the sea.

I will blow myself out given the chance
for whenever I mate with an ocean

there is a wake that leaves catastrophe.

Captives

She fills the corner, allows her little one
centre stage.

Her beggar bold eyes hold mine
for what seems an age

and when she releases me from her gaze,
she stares into middle-distance

as if calculating the sum of our difference.

I consider her drooped breasts,
more like a gran's than mother's

and her body is lumbered with cramps
when she stirs.

We are both female but there is a glitch
in my DNA.

I communicate with language.

Swift as a poacher's dart she rears
at the front of her cage.

A black whip arm loops her baby.
She goes back to her corner.

Flight

You said you'd come back as a bird
and find me
so I walked with my face
tipped to the sky.
Knowing your ways,
I kept an eye on jackdaws
until mid-summer's day
when a wing-beat quivered the air
and you rose from the farm gate;
hovered.

Under your shadow I stilled
and the burn of a glare scorched me.
My ears lengthened to strain silence.
A wind-waft of breath, blood-red,
twitched my nose with its rawness.

Fur wrapped me from back to belly
and the thump of my heart
kick-started my feet
towards the damp heat
of a burrow.